SO-BNZ-788

sendmail
Desktop Reference

sendmail
Desktop Reference

Bryan Costales and Eric Allman

sendmail Desktop Reference

by Bryan Costales and Eric Allman

Copyright © 1997 O'Reilly & Associates. All rights reserved.
Printed in the United States of America.

Editor: Gigi Estabrook

Production Editor: Clairemarie Fisher O'Leary

Printing History:
      April 1997:   First Edition.

Nutshell Handbook and the Nutshell Handbook logo are
registered trademarks of O'Reilly & Associates, Inc.

While every precaution has been taken in the preparation of
this book, the publisher assumes no responsibility for errors or
omissions, or for damages resulting from the use of the
information contained herein.

This book is printed on acid-free paper with 85% recycled
content, 15% post-consumer waste. O'Reilly & Associates is
committed to using paper with the highest recycled content
available consistent with high quality.

ISBN: 1-56592-278-6

Table of Contents

Preface

V8.8 Specific

The *sendmail* program is a Mail Transport Agent (MTA). It accepts mail from Mail User Agents (MUAs), mail users (humans), and other MTAs. It then delivers that mail to Mail Delivery Agents (MDAs) on the local machine, or transports that mail to another MTA at another machine. The behavior of *sendmail* is determined by its command line and by commands in its configuration file.

The *sendmail* program is written and maintained by Eric Allman at *sendmail.org*. Versions V8.7 and earlier are no longer supported and are no longer considered secure. If you are not currently running V8.8, we recommend you upgrade now. This Desktop Reference covers *sendmail* version 8.8.5.

This Desktop Reference is a companion to the second edition of the *sendmail* book by Bryan Costales with Eric Allman, published by O'Reilly & Associates. Section numbers herein reference the section numbers in that book. This is a reference guide only—for detail or tutorial information, refer to the full *sendmail* book.

Conventions

Bold   Denotes that you enter the text literally.

Italic   Means variable text, i.e., things you must fill in.

`Constant width`
          Is a keyword with a special meaning.

this(1)   Refers to the online manual for a program.

[...]   Denotes a range of optional selections you may
          make.

1

How to Run

The *sendmail* program is run by specifying its name followed by command-line switches, then recipient addresses. Some command-line switches cause *sendmail* to ignore its recipients, while others require their presence. One switch, **-bt**, places *sendmail* into interactive, rule-testing mode.

Alternative Names for sendmail

hoststat Prints persistent host status information (see §36.1.1).

mailq Prints the queue's contents (see §36.1.2).

newaliases
Rebuilds the *aliases* database file or files (see §36.1.3).

purgestat
Purges (zeroes) persistent host status information (see §36.1.4).

smtpd Runs in daemon mode (see §36.1.5).

Command-Line Switches

-B 7bit
Causes *sendmail* to clear the high-bit of every incoming byte, or **8bitmime**, which causes *sendmail* to preserve the high-bit (see §36.7.1).

-ba	Uses ARPAnet/Grey-Book protocols to transfer mail (see §36.7.3).
-bD	Runs as a daemon (just as with **-bd** below), but doesn't fork and doesn't detach from the controlling terminal (see §36.7.4).
-bd	Forks, detaches from the controlling terminal, and runs as a daemon, listening for incoming SMTP connections and handling them as they arrive (see §36.7.5).
-bH	Purges (zeroes) persistent host status information (see §36.7.6).
-bh	Prints persistent host status information (see §36.7.7).
-bi	Initializes the *aliases*(5) databases (see §24.5.1).
-bm	(The default) causes *sendmail* to read a message from its standard input and to send the read message (see §36.7.9).
-bp	Prints the contents of the queue (see §23.4).
-bs	Runs SMTP on standard I/O (see §36.7.11).
-bt	Runs in rule-testing mode (see 38.1).
-bv *root bob*	Verifies the addresses *root* and *bob* (see §36.7.13).
-C */tmp/test.cf*	Uses */tmp/test.cf* as its configuration file (see §36.7.15).
-c	Sets the `HoldExpensive` option to true (see §34.8.29).
-d0.4	Debugging mode to facility *0*, level *4* (see §37.1).
-F *'Jolly Roger'*	Sets the sender's full name to *Jolly Roger* (see §36.7.20).

-f *news@our.domain*

> Sets sender's address to *news@our.domain* (see §36.7.21).

-h *20*   Sets the minimum hop count to *20* (see §36.7.22).

-i   Sets the `IgnoreDots` option to true (see §36.7.24).

-M*rUUCP*

> Gives the macro **$r** the value *UUCP* (see §31.2).

-m   Sets the `MeToo` option to true (see §34.8.39).

-N never

> Says to never return DSN NOTIFY information when a message bounces (see §36.7.28). Can also be -N`success,failure,delay` to give notification on successful delivery, failed delivery, or delayed delivery.

-n   Suppresses aliasing (see §24.6).

-O*MaxQueueRunSize=100*

> Sets the `MaxQueueRunSize` option to *100* (see §34.1.2).

-o*Q/tmp*

> Sets the `QueueDirectory` option to */tmp* (see §34.1.1).

-p*UUCP:sonya*

> Sets the protocol stored in the **$r** macro to *UUCP* and the host stored in the **$s** macro to *sonya* (see §36.7.32).

-q*30m*   Runs *sendmail* in the background, waking up once every *30* minutes to process the queue (see §23.6.1).

-qR*@aol.com*

> Processes the queue once, delivering to all recipients in any queued message that contains at least one recipient at *aol.com* (see §23.6.2.3).

-R hdrs

Bounces only the headers of a message. **-Rfull** bounces headers and body (see §36.7.34).

-r   Is a (deprecated) synonym for **-f**.

-s   Sets the SaveFromLine option to true (deprecated, see §34.8.59).

-T 5d   Sets the Timeout.queuereturn option to 5 days (see §34.8.52).

-t   Gathers the list of recipients from the message's headers (see §36.7.38).

-U   Makes this the initial MUA to MTA submission (see §36.7.39).

-V cookie9167B5AS34

Sets the DSN ENVID string to cookie9167B5AS34 (see §36.7.40).

-v   Runs in verbose mode (see §36.7.41).

-X /var/tmp/smtp.trace

Logs both sides of all SMTP transactions to the /var/tmp/smtp.trace file (see §26.4).

Some Handy Debugging Switches

-v   When combined with **-d**, causes some otherwise lost debugging information to be printed.

-bD   Holds the *sendmail* daemon in the foreground so that **-d** debugging information about the running daemon can be viewed.

-d0   Shows the general configuration of your system: **-d0.1** prints version information (§37.5.1); **-d0.4** prints the local hostname and any aliases found for it (§37.5.2); **-d0.15** prints a list of the delivery agents declared (§37.5.4); and **-d0.20** prints the address of each network interface found (§37.5.5).

-d8   Traces most DNS lookups: **-d8.1** prints failure of the
              low-level MX search (§37.5.30); **-d8.2** prints calls to
              getcanonname(3) (§37.5.31); **-d8.3** traces dropped
              local hostnames (§37.5.32); **-d8.5** shows hostnames
              being tried in *getcanonname*(3) (§37.5.33); and
              -d8.8 shows when MX lookups get the wrong type
              (§37.5.35).

-d11   Traces delivery agent calls: **-d11.1** traces arguments
              passed to the delivery agent (§37.5.44); and **-d11.2**
              prints the user ID that the delivery agent is being
              invoked as (§37.5.45).

-d21   Traces rewriting of addresses: **-d21.1** traces general
              rule set rewriting (§37.5.67); **-d21.2** traces use of the
              $& macro (§37.5.68); **-d21.3** shows **$>** subroutines
              being called (§37.5.69); **-d21.4** displays the result of
              rewriting (§37.5.70); **-d21.15** shows **$***digit* replace-
              ment (§37.5.73); and **-d21.35** shows token-by-token
              LHS matching (§37.5.74).

-d27   Traces aliasing: **-d27.1** traces general aliasing
              (§37.5.88); **-d27.2** traces `:include:` files, alias self-
              references, and errors on home (§37.5.89); **-d27.3**
              traces trying the ˜/.*forward* path and the alias wait
              (§37.5.90); **-d27.4** prints "not safe" when a file is
              unsafe to trust (§37.5.91); and **-d27.9** shows *uid/gid*
              changes that correspond to `:include:` file reads
              (§37.5.94).

-d35   Traces macros: **-d35.9** shows macro values being
              defined (§37.5.120); **-d35.14** shows macro names
              being converted to integer identifiers (§37.5.121);
              and **-d35.24** shows macro expansion (§37.5.122).

-d37   Traces options and class macros: **-d37.1** traces the
              setting of options (§37.5.126); and **-d37.8** traces the
              adding of words to a class (§37.5.127).

-d41	Traces the queue: **-d41.1** traces queue ordering (§37.5.144); **-d41.2** shows failure to open *qf* files (37.5.145); **-d41.49** shows excluded (skipped) queue files (§37.5.146); and **-d41.50** shows every file in the queue (§37.5.147).
-d48	Traces the check_ rule sets: **-d48.2** traces calls to the check_ rule sets (§37.5.165).

Rule-Testing Mode (−bt) Commands

?	Prints help.

.D*rUUCP*
      Defines macro **$r** as *UUCP* (see §38.2.1).

.C*wlocalhost*
      Adds *localhost* to class **$=w** (see §38.2.2).

=S*5*	Dumps the contents of rule set *5* (see §38.4.1).
=M	Displays a list of the known delivery agents (see §38.4.2).
-d*48.2*	Sets debugging output to category *48* and level *2* (see §37.1).

${envid} Prints the value in the macro *{envid}* (see §38.3.1).

$=*w* Prints the contents of class macro **$=w** (see §38.3.2).

/mx *aol.com*
      Returns the MX records for *aol.com*, sorted into the order they will be tried, with equal cost records randomized (see §38.5.2).

/parse *bob*
      Parses the address *bob*, and returns the value of *crackaddr*( ) and the final parsed address including the selected delivery agent (see §38.5.5).

/try *local bob*
      Rewrites the address *bob* based on the rule sets indicated in the *local* delivery agent (see §38.5.6).

/tryflags *ER*

Sets flags used by **/parse** and **/try** to envelope recipient (see §38.5.4). Use E or H to choose envelope versus header, and R or S to choose recipient versus sender.

/canon *foo*

Transforms the hostname *foo* into its canonical form (see §38.5.1).

/map *aliases root*

Looks up *root* in the *aliases* database (see §38.5.3).

3,0 bob@foo

Runs the address *bob@foo* first through rule set 3, then rule set 0 (see §38.6).

Hints

/usr/lib/sendmail -bv *list* **| grep -v deliverable**

Causes *sendmail* to recursively expand the addresses in the mailing list named *list.* The –v with *grep*(1) causes all good (deliverable) addresses to be excluded and only bad addresses to be printed.

/usr/iib/sendmail -bt -d0.4 </dev/null

Causes *sendmail* to print its version, the #defines used when it was compiled, and how it is interpreting the identity of the local machine.

mailq -OMaxQueueRunSize=1

Allows *sendmail* to quickly print how many messages are queued even when the queue contains thousands of messages.

/usr/lib/sendmail -q -OTimeout.queuereturn=99d

Flushes messages from an old queue (perhaps following a prolonged downtime) while preventing old messages from timing out in the queue.

2

The sendmail.cf File

The *sendmail* configuration file, usually called *sendmail.cf*, provides all the central information that controls the *sendmail* program's behavior. It lists the location of all the other files *sendmail* needs to access and the location of all the directories in which *sendmail* needs to create and remove files. It sets the definitions *sendmail* uses when rewriting addresses. It defines the rules and sets of rules *sendmail* uses for transforming mail addresses (and aliases for those addresses) into usable information, such as which delivery agent to use and the correct form of the address to use with that delivery agent.

Overview

Each line in the configuration files begins with a key character that defines the function of that line. Any character other than those shown here is an error.

\#   Begins a comment line (the entire line is ignored).

tab   Continues the previous line.

space   Continues the previous line.

Cw *localhost*
            Adds *localhost* to class **w** (see §32.5.8).

C{GuestDomains} *guest.com visit.com*
            Adds *guest.com* and *visit.com* to the multi-character class named {**GuestDomains**} (see §32.1.1).

Dm*our.domain*

> Defines macro **m** with the value *our.domain* (see §31.10.24).

D{OurOldDomain} *old.domain*

> Defines multi-character macro name {OurOld-Domain} with the value *old.domain* (see §31.3).

EHOME=*/u/mail*

> Assigns value */u/mail* to the environmental variable HOME. (Such assignments are only available to delivery agents that *sendmail* executes.) (See 22.2.1.)

EUSER   Imports the value of USER from the environment and makes it available to delivery agents.

Fw */etc/sendmail.cw*

> Fills the class **w** with values read from the */etc/sendmail.cw* file (see §19.6.26).

Fk │*/usr/sbin/showuu*

> Runs the program */usr/sbin/showuu* and fills the class **k** with values printed by that program. (see §32.5.2).

HDate: *$a*

> Defines the Date: header with the value *$a* (see §35.10.10).

H?P?Return-Path: *<$g>*

> Defines the Return-Path: header with the value *<$g>*. This header will only be output if the **P** in ?P? appears in the delivery agent's **F=** equate (see §35.4).

K*uid text −z: −k2 −v0 /etc/passwd*

> Declares a database named *uid* to be of class *text*, which will look up keys in the flat file named */etc/passwd* (see §33.8.18). The *−z:*, *−k2*, and *−v0* say that */etc/passwd* has colon-delimited fields, that the key will be in the index 2 field, and the value in the

index 0 field, thus converting *uid* values to login names, see §33.3.4.12).

M*name, equate=value,* ...

Declares a mail delivery agent. The *name* is the symbolic name for this agent. The items in the *equate* list are described in the next section, "Delivery Agent Equates."

O MaxQueueRunSize=*100*

Gives the option MaxQueueRunSize the value *100* (see §34.8.38). Note that there must be a space between the **O** and the option name. Options are summarized later in this chapter.

O*J/var/forward/$u:$z/.forward*

Uses the old single-character name *J* to define the *ForwardPath* option (see §34.8.27).

Pbulk=*–60*

Associates the symbolic name bulk with a delivery priority of *–60.* These symbolic names are compared to the Precedence: header (if one) during delivery, and used to begin a message's priority in the queue (see §35.8).

RLHS *tabs* RHS [*tabs* COMMENT]

Defines a rewriting rule (do-while clause) where the RHS rewrites an address while the LHS comparison evaluates to true. The LHS and RHS must be separated by one or more *tab* characters. Optional *tabs* and a COMMENT may follow and are not part of the rewriting rule (see §28.1).

S*name*[*=val*]

Declares a rule-set start to have the name *name* (where *name* is either a number or is symbolic text). When *name* is symbolic, an optional numeric value *val* may be assigned to it (see §29.1).

T *bob jane*

> Declares that the users *bob* and *jane* are "trusted"
> and may use the -f command-line switch to precon-
> dition the sender identity. Users who are not trusted
> and who use the -f switch cause a warning to be
> included in the outgoing mail headers (see §22.8.1).

V *7/Berkeley*

> Specifies the version of the configuration file to be 7.
> An optional slash and a vendor identifier may fol-
> low, as */Berkeley* (see §27.5).

Delivery Agent Equates

The general form of a delivery agent's declaration looks like
this:

    M*name*, *equate=val*, ...

In this section we list and describe each *equate*, where only
the first letter of each is recognized (that is, **Argv=** is the same
as **A=**).

A= *argv0 argv1* . . .

> Lists the delivery agent's command-line arguments.
> The delivery agent speaks SMTP only if **$u** is absent
> from those arguments. The special symbolic *argv0*
> names IPC and LPC reference internal *sendmail* code.

C= *ISO-8859-1*

> Uses the *ISO-8859-1* character set in the MIME Con-
> tent-Type: header (see §30.4.2). Applies to mes-
> sages received *from* this delivery agent. Supersedes
> the **DefaultCharSet** option.

D= */var/run:/tmp*

> Sets the paths for execution of the **prog** delivery
> agent to */var/run* first, and if it cannot *chdir*(2) into
> that directory, then to */tmp* (see §30.4.3).

E=\r   Specifies the end-of-line characters to be a carriage-return newline pair. Those characters are generated by *sendmail* for outgoing messages and recognized by *sendmail* for incoming messages. The default is \r\n for SMTP and \n otherwise (see §30.4.4).

F=_flags_   Lists *flags* that describe a delivery agent's behavior (fully listed in the next section, "Delivery Agent F= Flags").

L=_512_   Limits the length of text lines in the body of a mail message to *512* characters (see §30.4.6).

M=_1000000_

Limits the total size (header and body combined) of messages handled by the delivery agent to one million characters.

N=_5_   Says to re-*nice*(2) the delivery agent by *5* (see §30.4.8).

P=_/usr/bin/uux_

Says to execute */usr/bin/uux* as the delivery-agent program (see §30.4.9). Special symbolic paths can also be used: [IPC] makes a network connection and speaks SMTP; [FILE] appends the message to a file; and [LPC] is useful for tracking down mail problems.

R=_rset_ or **R=**_eset/hset_

Lists the rewriting rule set names or numbers for the recipient. A single name or number is applied to both envelope and header rewriting. Two names or numbers, separated by a slash, applies the leftmost to the envelope and the rightmost to headers (see §30.4.10).

S=_rset_ or **R=**_eset/hset_

Lists the rewriting rule set names or numbers for the sender. Particulars are the same as for **R=** above (see §30.4.11).

T=_DNS/RFC822/X-Unix_

Sets the type tags used in the DSN diagnostic returns for this delivery agent. The type tag for the `Reporting-MTA:` field is _DNS_; the type tag for the `Final-Recipient:` field is _RFC822_; and the type tag for the `Diagnostic-Code:` field is _X-Unix_ (see §30.4.12).

U=_nullmail:nullgroup_

Specifies that _sendmail_ should become the user _nullmail_ and the group _nullgroup_ before executing the delivery agent. If the _:nullgroup_ is omitted, it is found in the _passwd_(5) file entry for _nullmail_ (see §30.4.13).

Delivery Agent F= Flags

F=0	Turns off MX lookups for this delivery agent (see §30.8.1).
F=3	Extends quoted-printable conversions to encode ASCII characters that cannot be represented in EBCDIC (see §30.8.2).
F=5	Uses rule set 5 after local aliasing (see §30.8.3).
F=7	Strips the high bit when delivering (see §30.8.4).
F=8	Forces `EightBitMode=p` for this delivery agent (see §30.8.5).
F=:	Checks for `:include:` files (see §30.8.7).
F=|	Checks for |_program_ addresses (see §30.8.8).
F=/	Checks for /_file_ addresses (see §30.8.9).
F=@	Allows users to be looked up in the User Database (see §30.8.10).
F=a	Runs the extended SMTP protocol (see §30.8.11).

F=A	Allows users to be in the LHS of an alias (see §30.8.12).
F=b	Ensures a blank line after message (see §30.8.13).
F=c	Excludes comment from **$g** in headers (see §30.8.14).
F=C	Adds *@domain* to recipient that lacks one (see §30.8.15). Applies to the *sending* delivery agent only.
F=d	Never encloses route addresses in <> (see §30.8.16).
F=D	Specifies the need for a `Date:` header (see §30.8.17).
F=e	Marks this delivery agent as "expensive" (see §30.8.18).
F=E	Changes any extra lines that begin in "From" into ">From" (see §30.8.19).
F=f	Causes delivery agent to add –f to argv (see §30.8.20).
F=F	Specifies the need for a `From:` header (see §30.8.21).
F=g	Suppresses sending of `From:<>` senders in bounce messages (see §30.8.22).
F=h	Preserves uppercase in hostnames (see §30.8.23).
F=i	Specifies to perform a User Database rewrite on the envelope sender (see §30.8.24).
F=I	Causes delivery agent to send SMTP VERB to the other site (see §30.8.25).
F=j	Specifies to perform a User Database rewrite of header recipient addresses (see §30.8.26).
F=k	Suppresses check for loops in HELO command (see §30.8.27).

F=l	Specifies that delivery agent is local (final) delivery (see §30.8.28).
F=L	Causes SMTP line limits to be applied (obsolete, see §30.8.29).
F=m	Says that the delivery agent can deliver to multiple recipients at once (see §30.8.30).
F=M	Specifies the need for a `Message-ID:` header (see §30.8.31).
F=n	Prevents the addition of a UNIX mailbox-style `From` to headers (see §30.8.32).
F=o	Runs the delivery agent under the *uid* and *gid* of the recipient (see §30.8.33).
F=p	Attempts to process the return path correctly (deprecated, see §30.8.34).
F=P	Specifies the need for a `Return-Path:` header (see §30.8.35).
F=q	Says to use a 252 instead of a 250 return code for an SMTP VRFY reply (see §30.8.36).
F=r	Causes the delivery agent to add a –r to argv (see §30.8.37).
F=R	Tells *sendmail* to use a reserved TCP port (see §30.8.38).
F=s	Causes quotation marks to be stripped from addresses (see §30.8.39).
F=S	Always run the delivery agent under a *uid* and *gid* specified (see §30.8.40).
F=u	Preserves uppercase for user names (see §30.8.41).
F=U	Prepends a UUCP-style `From` line (see §30.8.42).
F=w	Verifies that the user is local by checking for an */etc/passwd* entry (see §30.8.43).

F=x   Specifies that the delivery agent requires a Full-Name: header (see §30.8.44).

F=X   Specifies that the delivery agent needs an RFC821 hidden dot (see §30.8.45).

Defined Macros

Defined macros allow strings of text to be represented symbolically. A defined macro is one whose symbol represents a single string.

>   D*Xstring*

The symbolic name (here *X*) is either a single letter or a multi-character name. If multi-character, it must be surrounded by curly braces:

>   D*{XXX}string*

The value in a defined macro is referenced by prefixing its name with a **$**. Because defined macros in rules are expanded when the configuration file is read, a **$&** prefix can be used when deferred expansion is desired.

The *sendmail* program reserves all macros but those beginning with an uppercase letter for its own internal use. Since the *m4* configuration technique is not internal (to the program), it uses uppercase macro names. Here we show the internal macros currently used by *sendmail* and the external macros currently used by the *m4* technique.

$_   Holds the RFC1413-validation text, and any IP source route information that was found (see §31.10.1).

$a   Contains the origin date in RFC822 format (see §31.10.2).

$b   Contains the current date in RFC822 format (see §31.10.3).

${bodytype}

> Contains the ESMTP BODY parameter for the current message (see §31.10.4).

$B Specifies the BITNET relay (see §31.10.5). This macro can be set using the *m4* technique by defining BITNET_RELAY.

$c Contains the current hop count (see §31.10.6).

${client_addr}

> Stores the current connecting host's IP address (see §31.10.7).

${client_name}

> Stores the current connecting host's canonical name (see §31.10.8).

$C Specifies the hostname of the DECnet relay (see §31.10.9). This macro can be set using the *m4* technique by defining DECNET_RELAY.

$d Contains the current date in UNIX *ctime*(3) format (see §31.10.10).

${envid} Holds the original DSN envelope ID (see §31.10.12).

$E Specifies the X.400 relay (unused, see §31.10.13).

$f Contains the current sender's (the From:) address (see §31.10.14).

$F Specifies the FAX relay (see §31.10.15). This macro can be set using the *m4* technique by defining FAX_RELAY.

$g Contains the current sender's address relative to the recipient (see §31.10.16).

$h Contains the host part of the current recipient address (see §31.10.17).

$H Specifies the mail hub (see §31.10.18). This macro can be set using the *m4* technique by defining MAIL_HUB.

$i	Contains the queue identifier for the current message (see §31.10.19).
$j	Holds the official canonical name of the local machine (see §31.10.20). This macro can be set using the *m4* technique by defining `confDOMAIN_NAME`.
$k	Holds the UUCP name of the local machine (see §31.10.21).
$L	Specifies the "local user" relay (see §31.10.23). This macro can be set using the *m4* technique by defining `LUSER_RELAY`.
$m	Holds the official domain name for the local machine (see §31.10.24).
$M	Specifies who we are masquerading as (see §31.10.25). This macro can be set using the *m4* technique using the `MASQUERADE_AS` construct.
$n	Specifies whom error messages should be from (see §31.10.26). This macro can be set using the *m4* technique by defining `confMAILER_NAME`.
${opMode}	Contains the operating mode that *sendmail* started in (see §31.10.28).
$p	Contains the current *sendmail* process' *pid* (see §31.10.29).
$r	Contains the protocol used to receive the current message (see §31.10.31).
$R	Specifies the relay for user names that lack an *@host.domain* part (see §31.10.32). This macro can be set using the *m4* technique by defining `LOCAL_RELAY`.
$s	Contains the current sender host's name (see §31.10.33).

$S	Specifies the Smart Host (see §31.10.34). This macro can be set using the *m4* technique by defining SMART_HOST.
$t	Contains the current time in seconds (see §31.10.35).
$u	Contains the current recipient's user name (can be auto-replicated in the **A=** equate of a delivery agent if **F=m** is present) (see §31.10.36).
$U	Specifies the UUCP name to override **$k** (see §31.10.37).
$v	Holds the *sendmail* program's version (see §31.10.38).
$V	Specifies the UUCP relay (for the class **$=V**) (see §31.10.39).
$w	Holds the short name of the local host (see §31.10.40).
$W	Specifies the UUCP relay (for the class **$=W**) (see §31.10.41).
$x	Contains the "full name" of the current sender (see §31.10.42).
$X	Specifies the UUCP relay (for the class **$=X**) (see §31.10.43).
$y	Holds the name of the controlling tty (see §31.10.44).
$Y	Specifies the UUCP relay for unclassified hosts (see §31.10.45).
$z	Contains the current recipient's home directory (see §31.10.46).
$Z	Specifies the version of this *m4* configuration (see §31.10.47). This macro can be appended to using the *m4* technique by defining confCF_VERSION.

Class Macros

A class macro is one whose symbol can represent multiple words. Those words can be declared in the configuration line or read from an external file or from the output of an executed program.

    CXword word ...
    FX /file
    FX |program

The symbolic name (here *X*) is either a single letter or a multi-character name. If multi-character, it must be surrounded by curly braces:

    C{XXX}word word ...
    F{XXX} /file
    F{XXX} |program

The *sendmail* program reserves all but class names that begin with an uppercase letter for its own internal use. Class macros are usable only in the LHS of rules. A **$=** prefix matches a token to any *word* in the class. A **$~** prefix matches if the token is not in the class.

$=e Determines whether or not a `Content-Transfer-Encoding:` type will be quoted-printable encoded. The default contents for this class are `7bit`, `8bit`, and `binary` (see §32.5.1).

$=k Lists the UUCP names of the local host (see §32.5.2).

$=m Lists all the known domain names for the local host. Available to rule sets but not currently used by the *m4* technique (see §32.5.3).

$=n Determines the `Content-Type:` headers that are prevented from being converted from 8- to 7-bits. The default content for this class is `multipart/signed` (see §32.5.4).

$=q	Determines the `Content-Type:` headers that should not be converted from from 8- to 7-bits with base64 encoding. By default this class is empty (see §32.5.5).
$=s	Lists `Content-Type:` header `message` subtypes that should be treated the same as `rfc822`. By default this list contains only `rfc822` (see §32.5.6).
$=t	Lists "trusted" users who may specify an alternative sender with the `-f` command-line switch (see §32.5.7).
$=w	Lists all the hostnames by which the local host can be known. Either found by *sendmail* at startup, or declared in the configuration file, or listed in the *sendmail.cw* file (see §32.5.8).

Options

Options determine most of the *sendmail* program's behavior. They are declared on the command line with the -O switch:

    -Oname=value

and in the configuration file with the O line:

    O name=value

The space following the O is mandatory. Prior to V8.7 *sendmail*, option names could be only a single character. Beginning with V8.7, option names can be multi-character. Where appropriate, the old form is listed parenthetically after the new form.

True/False options, when absent, default to false, but when present with no value, default to true. Options marked as "(safe)" can be specified on the command line without giving up root privileges.

AliasFile=*file*[*,file*, ...]

Defines the location (and optionally the type as *type:file*) of the *aliases* file or files. (Was the **A** option, see §34.8.1, or define ALIAS_FILE with the *m4* technique.)

AliasWait=*interval*

Specifies the *interval sendmail* will wait for the *aliases* database to rebuild. (Was the **a** option, see §34.8.2, or define confALIAS_WAIT with the *m4* technique.)

AllowBogusHELO=[*True*|*False*]

(safe) allows *sendmail* to accept an SMTP HELO or EHLO that is not followed by a hostname (see §34.8.3).

AutoRebuildAliases=[*True*|*False*]

Allows *sendmail* to automatically rebuild the *aliases* database. (Was the **D** option, see §34.8.4, or define confAUTO_REBUILD with the *m4* technique.)

BlankSub=*char*

Specifies the unquoted space replacement character *char*. (Was the **B** option, see §34.8.5, or define confBLANK_SUB with the *m4* technique.)

CheckAliases=[*True*|*False*]

(safe) tells *sendmail* to check the right side of aliases in the *aliases* file in addition to the normal left side checks. (Was the **n** option, see §34.8.6, or define confCHECK_ALIASES with the *m4* technique.)

CheckpointInterval=*number*

States the *number* of recipients that will be delivered between checkpoints (flushes to disk) of the *qf* file. (Was the **C** option, see §34.8.7, or define confCHECKPOINT_INTERVAL with the *m4* technique.)

ClassFactor=*factor*

> Sets the multiplication *factor* for calculating priority increments. (Was the **z** option, see §34.8.8, or define `confWORK_CLASS_FACTOR` with the *m4* technique.)

ColonOkInAddr=[*True*|*False*]

> (safe) tells *sendmail* to allow colons in addresses, thus disabling recognition of `:;` list addresses— DECnet `::` is always allowed (see §34.8.9, or define `confCOLON_OK_IN_ADDR` with the *m4* technique).

ConnectionCacheSize=*number*

> Stipulates the *number* of simultaneous open SMTP connections *sendmail* will maintain during delivery. (Was the **k** option, see §34.8.10, or define `confMCI_CACHE_SIZE` with the *m4* technique.)

ConnectionCacheTimeout=*duration*

> Stipulates the *duration* of time any given open, but when idle, SMTP connection will be maintained. (Was the **K** option, see §34.8.11, or define `confMCI_CACHE_ TIMEOUT` with the *m4* technique.)

ConnectionRateThrottle=*number*

> Specifies the maximum *number* of incoming connections that will be accepted per second. Additional connections are accepted progressively more slowly (see §34.8.12, or define `confCONNECTION_ RATE_THROTTLE` with the *m4* technique).

DaemonPortOptions=*option=value*[,*option=value,* ...]

> Sets the daemon TCP/IP port options. Available *options* are: `Addr` is the network to accept connections from; `Family` is the type of network; `Listen` is the size of the *listen*(2) queue; `Port` is the port on which *sendmail* should listen; `ReceiveSize` is the size of the TCP/IP receive buffer; and `SendSize` is the size of the TCP/IP send buffer. (Was the **O**

---

option, see §34.8.13, or define confDAEMON_
OPTIONS with the *m4* technique.)

DefaultCharSet=*set*

(safe) Defines the character *set* that will be listed in
the Content-Type: header, for MIME 8- to 7-bit
conversion (see §34.8.14, or define confDEF_CHAR_
SET with the *m4* technique).

DefaultUser=*user*[:*group*]

Specifies the default non-*root* identity for *sendmail*.
The *user* may be a numeric *uid* or a login name. If
group is omitted, *user* is looked up in the *passwd*(5)
database, and that *gid* is used. Otherwise, *group*
may be a numeric *gid* or a group name. (Was the **u**
and **g** options, see §34.8.15, or define confDEF_
USER_ID with the *m4* technique.)

DeliveryMode=*mode*

(safe) sets the delivery *mode* that *sendmail* will run
as. Select *mode* from: background to run asyn-
chronously; interactive to run synchronously;
queue-only to queue, rather than deliver, all mail;
or deferred to queue all mail *without* doing any
DNS lookups. (Was the **d** option, see §34.8.16, or
define confDELIVERY_MODE with the *m4* technique.)

DialDelay=*interval*

Specifies how long to sleep after a connection failure. If non-zero, sleeps that *interval* then tries again
(see §34.8.17, or define confDIAL_DELAY with the
m4 technique).

DontExpandCnames=[*True*|*False*]

(safe) prevents CNAME expansion when looking up
MX records (see §34.8.18, or define confDONT_
EXPAND_CNAMES with the *m4* technique).

DontInitGroups=[*True*| *False*]

> Suppresses use of the *initgroups*(3) call to look up additional group memberships (see §34.8.19, or define `confDONT_INIT_GROUPS` with the *m4* technique).

DontPruneRoutes=[*True*| *False*]

> Prevents *sendmail* from short-circuiting source routes. (Was the **R** option, see §34.8.20, or define `confDONT_PRUNE_ROUTES` with the *m4* technique.)

DoubleBounceAddress= *address*

> Specifies the *address* to which an error message should be sent if there is an error sending an error message (see §34.8.21, or define `confDOU-BLE_BOUNCE_ADDRESS` with the *m4* technique).

EightBitMode= *how*

> (safe) specifies how to convert unlabeled MIME input. Select from: `mimify` to force conversion of 8BITMIME to 7-bit; `pass` to pass unlabeled 8-bit input through as-is; or `strict` to reject unlabeled 8-bit input. (Was the **8** option, see §34.8.22, or define `confEIGHT_BIT_HANDLING` with the *m4* technique.)

ErrorHeader= *description*

> (safe) specifies text or a file's contents to insert at the top of bounced messages. If the *description* starts with a slash, it is taken as the full pathname of a file, otherwise the *description* is taken as literal text. The text is macro-expanded during interpolation. (Was the **E** option, see §34.8.23, or define `confERROR_MESSAGE` with the *m4* technique.)

ErrorMode= *mode*

> Specify *mode* of error handling. Select from: `m` to mail error notification to the sender no matter what; `e` to act just like `m`, but to always exit with a zero

exit status; p to print error messages (the default); q
to remain silent about all delivery errors; or w to
write errors to the sender's terminal screen. (Was
the **e** option, see §34.8.24, or define confERROR_
MODE with the *m4* technique.)

FallbackMXhost=_host_

Specifies the *host* to send mail to when all connec-
tions to the actual MX hosts have failed. (Was the **V**
option, see §34.8.25, or define confFALLBACK_MX
with the *m4* technique.)

ForkEachJob=[*True* | *False*]

Causes queue files to be processed individually to
lessen the impact on small-memory machines. (Was
the **Y** option, see §34.8.26, or define
confSEPARATE_PROC with the *m4* technique.)

ForwardPath=_file_[*, file, . . .*]

Sets the `~/.forward` search path. Each *file* name is
macro-expanded, then tried. Each is tried in turn
until one can be read, whereupon it is the `~/.for-
ward` for that local recipient. (Was the **J** option, see
§34.8.27, or define confFORWARD_PATH with the
m4 technique.)

HelpFile=_file_

Specifies the location of the *file* that contains help
messages for the SMTP (and ESMTP) HELP command,
and usage for the **-bt** rule-testing command. (Was
the **H** option, see §34.8.28, or define HELP_FILE
with the *m4* technique.)

HoldExpensive=[*True* | *False*]

Tells *sendmail* to queue rather than deliver messages that will be delivered by "expensive" delivery
agents (those with an **F=e** flag set). (Was the **c**
option, see §34.8.29, or define confCON_
EXPENSIVE with the *m4* technique.)

HostsFile=*file*

> Specifies an alternative for the */etc/hosts file* (see
> §34.8.30, or define confHOSTS_FILE with the *m4*
> technique).

HostStatusDirectory=*directory*

> Specifies the *directory* in which *sendmail* should
> store persistent host status. If specified, this also
> enables the keeping of that status. A relative name is
> relative to the queue directory (see §34.8.31, or
> define confHOST_STATUS_DIRECTORY with the
> *m4* technique).

IgnoreDots=[*True*| *False*]

> (safe) tells *sendmail* to ignore leading dots in the
> message body. (Was the i option, see §34.8.32, or
> define confIGNORE_DOTS with the *m4* technique.)

LogLevel=*level*

> (safe) sets the logging *level*, where a level of: 0-6
> logs progressively less serious problems; 7 logs
> delivery failures; 8 logs delivery successes; 9 logs
> deferred delivery; 10-11 logs database and *nis*
> lookups; 12 logs all incoming and outgoing SMTP
> commands; 13 logs questionable permissions; and
> 14-98 logs progressively more detailed debugging
> information. On the command line, you can only
> increase the logging level. (Was the L option, see
> §34.8.33, or define confLOG_LEVEL with the *m4*
> technique.)

MatchGECOS=[*True*| *False*]

> Enables so called "Fuzzy" matching of the recipient
> in the *gecos* field of the *passwd*(5) database. (Was
> the G option, see §34.8.34, or define confMATCH_
> GECOS with the *m4* technique.)

MaxDaemonChildren=*number*

> Specifies maximum *number* of children that *send-
> mail* will fork to process inbound connections. Does

---

not limit forked children that process the queue (see §34.8.35, or define confMAX_DAEMON_CHILDREN with the *m4* technique).

MaxHopCount=*number*

Sets the maximum *number* of times a message may be relayed through mail-handling sites (the maximum hop count). (Was the **h** option, see §34.8.36, or define confMAX_HOP with the *m4* technique.)

MaxMessageSize=*size*

Specifies the maximum *size* (in bytes) of an incoming message that *sendmail* will accept (see §34.8.37, or define confMAX_MESSAGE_SIZE with the *m4* technique).

MaxQueueRunSize=*number*

(safe) specifies the maximum *number* of queued messages that *sendmail* will process from a queue in a given queue run (see §34.8.38, or define confMAX_QUEUE_RUN_SIZE with the *m4* technique).

MeToo=[*True***|***False***]**

(safe) causes a copy of the message to be sent to the sender too, when the sender is one of the recipients listed in an alias or mailing list. (Was the **m** option, see §34.8.39, or define confME_TOO with the *m4* technique.)

MinFreeBlocks=*number*

(safe) defines minimum *number* of free disk blocks that must be available when a message's size is stated with the SIZE keyword to the ESMTP MAIL command. (Was the **b** option, see §34.8.40, or define confMIN_FREE_BLOCKS with the *m4* technique.)

MinQueueAge=*interval*

(safe) skips processing of a queued file if the last time it was processed is sooner than the *interval*

specified (see §34.8.41, or define confMIN_
QUEUE_AGE with the *m4* technique).

MustQuoteChars=*characters*

Allows *sendmail* to quote nonaddress *characters* in
an address, as required by RFC822 (see §34.8.42).

NoRecipientAction=*how*

(safe) specifies *how* to handle the situation of no
recipients being specified in the header (as would
be the case when all recipients were specified in
Bcc: headers). Select from: add-appar-
ently-to, which adds an Apparently-To:
header; add-bcc, which adds an empty Bcc:
header; add-to, which adds an empty To: header;
add-undisclosed, which adds a To: undis-
closed-recipients:; header; or none, which
passes the message unchanged (see §34.8.43, or
define confNO_RCPT_ACTION with the *m4* technique).

OldStyleHeaders=[*True|False***]**

(safe) causes *sendmail* to insert commas between
the recipients listed in a space-delimited list of
recipients. (Was the o option, see §34.8.44, or
define confOLD_STYLE_HEADERS with the *m4*
technique.)

OperatorChars=*characters*

Sets token-separation operators to the list of *characters* given. (Was the $o macro, see §34.8.45, or
define confOPERATORS with the *m4* technique.)

PostmasterCopy=*address*

Enables the user, whose email *address* is given, to
receive an extra copy of every bounce message.
(Was the P option, see §34.8.46, or define
confCOPY_ERRORS_TO with the *m4* technique.)

PrivacyOptions=_option_[_,option, ...]_

(safe) increases privacy and security of the daemon. Each _option_ adds to earlier options. Select from: `authwarnings`, which enables X-Authentication-Warning: headers; `needexpnhelo`, which requires SMTP HELO before EXPN; `needmailhelo`, which requires SMTP HELO before MAIL; `needvrfyhelo`, which requires SMTP HELO before VRFY; `noexpn`, which disables all SMTP EXPN commands; `novrfy`, which disables all SMTP VRFY commands; and `goaway`, which enables all the preceding. Also select from: `public`, which means none of the preceding; `restrictmailq`, which restricts who may run _mailq_(1); `restrictqrun`, which restricts who may process the queue; and `noreceipts`, which disables sending of return-receipt mail. (Was the `p` option, see §34.8.47, or define `confPRIVACY_FLAGS` with the _m4_ technique.)

QueueDirectory=_pathname_

Specifies the full _pathname_ of the queue directory. (Was the **Q** option, see §34.8.48, or define `QUEUE_DIR` with the _m4_ technique.)

QueueFactor=_factor_

Sets the _factor_ for high-load queuing. When a message is received, the decision to deliver or to queue it is based on the formula:

```
priority > QueueFactor /
    (load - QueueLA + 1)
```

If the priority of the message is greater than the result of this formula, where `load` is the current load average, the message is delivered. (Was the **q** option, see §34.8.49, or define `confQUEUE_FACTOR` with the _m4_ technique.)

QueueLA=_load_

>Specifies the _load_ average above which queue runs will be skipped. This is also used in the formula shown above for **QueueFactor**. (Was the **x** option, see §34.8.50, or define `confQUEUE_LA` with the _m4_ technique.)

QueueSortOrder=_how_

>(safe) specifies _how_ to presort the queue. Select from: `host` to sort by recipient host, lock status, and priority; `priority` for a simple sort of the message priorities; or `time` to sort based on submission time (see §34.8.51, or define `confQUEUE_SORT_ORDER` with the _m4_ technique).

QueueTimeout=_interval_

>Limits the life of a queued message to the _interval_ specified. The first delivery failure after that interval is exceeded causes the message to bounce. (Was the **T** option; deprecated, use the `Timeout.queuereturn` option instead.)

RecipientFactor=_factor_

>Penalizes large recipient lists by multiplying the number of recipients by this _factor_ when determining a message's priority. (Was the **y** option, see §34.8.53, or define `confWORK_RECIPIENT_FACTOR` with the _m4_ technique.)

RefuseLA=_load_

>Tells _sendmail_ to refuse incoming SMTP connections when the _load_ average exceeds this specified load. (Was the **X** option, see §34.8.54, or define `confREFUSE_LA` with the _m4_ technique.)

ResolverOptions=_arg_ [_arg_ ...]

>Tunes DNS lookups by specifying an _arg_, or args, such as: `+AAONLY`, which turns on the AAONLY name server option (Authoritative Answers Only); and `-DNSRCH`, which turns off the DNSRCH name

server option (search the domain path). (Was the I option, see §34.8.55, or define confBIND_OPTS with the *m4* technique.)

RetryFactor=*increment*

Sets the amount to *increment* a job's priority each time a message fails to be delivered. (Was the Z option, see §34.8.56, or define confWORK_ TIME_FACTOR with the *m4* technique.)

RunAsUser=*user*[:*group*]

Runs *sendmail* as a *user* other than *root*. The *user* may be a numeric *uid* or a login name. If *group* is omitted, *user* is looked up in the *passwd*(5) database and the primary *gid* is used. Otherwise, *group* may be a numeric *gid* or a group name (see §34.8.57, or define confRUN_AS_USER with the *m4* technique).

SafeFileEnvironment=*pathname*

Sets the *pathname* to a directory that is safe for file writes. The *sendmail* program does a *chdir*(2) to that directory before writing to files. Also prevents writing to other than plain files, with the exception of */dev/null* (see §34.8.58, or define confSAFE_ FILE_ENV with the *m4* technique).

SaveFromLine=[*True*|*False*]

Prevents *sendmail* from removing UNIX mailbox-style **From** lines from input. (Was the f option, see §34.8.59, or define confSAVE_FROM_LINES with the *m4* technique.)

SendMimeErrors=[*True*|*False*]

(safe) Tells *sendmail* it may return error messages (bounced mail notifications) in MIME format. (Was the j option, see §34.8.60, or define confMIME_ FORMAT_ERRORS with the *m4* technique.)

ServiceSwitchFile=*file*

Specifies the location of the switched-services *file*. Under Solaris, DEC OSF/1, and Ultrix, this option is

---

ignored, and the system file automatically used. A switch-services file defines how and in what order services, such as alias, host, and user information, will be looked up (see §34.8.61, or define confSERVICE_SWITCH_FILE with the *m4* technique).

SevenBitInput=[*True*|*False*]

(safe) Forces *sendmail* to clear the high-bit of each byte of a message's body that it reads. (Was the 7 option, see §34.8.62, or define confSEVEN_BIT_INPUT with the *m4* technique.)

SingleLineFromHeader=[*True*|*False*]

(safe) Tells *sendmail* to strip all newline characters from From: headers (see §34.8.63).

SingleThreadDelivery=[*True*|*False*]

Ensures that only a single *sendmail* will ever be delivering to a given host at a given time. Requires that the HostStatusDirectory option be set (see §34.8.64, or define confSINGLE_THREAD_DELIVERY with the *m4* technique).

SmtpGreetingMessage=*$j Sendmail $v ready at $b*

Specifies the SMTP greeting message. (Was the $e macro, see §34.8.65, or define confSMTP_LOGIN_MSG with the *m4* technique.)

StatusFile=*file*

Specifies the location of the statistics *file* (usually *sendmail.st* preceded by an appropriate path). (Was the S option, see §34.8.66, or define STATUS_FILE with the *m4* technique.)

SuperSafe=[*True*|*False*]

(safe) Ensures additional reliability by forcing all messages to be queued, even if they could be directly delivered. (Was the s option, see §34.8.67, or define confSAFE_QUEUE with the *m4* technique.)

TempFileMode=_mode_

> Sets the default _permissions_ (in octal) for created temporary files. (Was the **F** option, see §34.8.68, or define conf TEMP_FILE_MODE with the _m4_ technique.)

TimeZoneSpec=_zone_

> Sets the time _zone_ to that specified. If _zone_ is absent, imports the TZ variable from the environment. If the entire option is missing, the default is to unset the TZ environmental variable and use the system default. (Was the **t** option, see §34.8.69, or define conf TIME_ZONE with the _m4_ technique.)

Timeout._event_=_interval_

> Sets the timeout for an _event_ to the _interval_ specified. See the section "The Timeout Option" for details.

TryNullMXList=[_True_|_False_]

> (safe) Tells _sendmail_ to connect directly to the A record for a host when the best MX record points to this host. (Was the **w** option, see §34.8.71, or define conf TRY_NULL_MX_LIST with the _m4_ technique.)

UnixFromLine=_format_

> Defines the _format_ for the UUCP-style From line. (Was the **$l** macro, see §34.8.72, or define conf FROM_LINE with the _m4_ technique.)

UnsafeGroupWrites=[_True_|_False_]

> Tells _sendmail_ to check group write permissions on files that it is taking addresses from, and to reject those files (and hence the addresses) when such group write permissions are found (see §34.8.73, or define conf UNSAFE_GROUP_WRITES with the _m4_ technique).

UseErrorsTo=[_True_|_False_]

> (safe) Allows error notification to be sent to the address listed in the Errors-To: header in

---

addition to that sent to the envelope sender. (Was
the l option, see §34.8.74, or define confUSE_
ERRORS_TO with the *m4* technique.)

UserDatabaseSpec=*file*

> Specifies the location of the database *file* that will be
> used for User Database lookups. (Was the U
> option, see §34.8.75, or define confUSERDB_SPEC
> with the *m4* technique.)

Verbose=[*True* | *False***]**

> (safe) Causes *sendmail* to run in verbose mode.
> (Was the v option, see §34.8.76.)

The Timeout Option

The Timeout option is used to set many internal timeouts.
Its general form looks like this:

    OTimeout.*event=interval*

Here we describe each *event*. Each *interval* is represented by
an integer followed by a unit of time: **s** for seconds; **m** for
minutes; **h** for hours; **d** for days; and **w** for weeks. They may
be chained, as for example:

    3d22h4s

sets an *interval* of 3 days, 22 hours, and 4 seconds.

Timeout.command=*interval*

> Sets the maximum *interval* of time to wait for arrival
> of the next anticipated SMTP command (see
> §34.8.70.1, or define confTO_COMMAND with the *m4*
> technique).

Timeout.connect=*interval*

> Sets the maximum *interval* to wait for the *connect*(2)
> system call to return (see §34.8.70.2, or define
> confTO_CONNECT with the *m4* technique).

Timeout.datablock=_interval_

> Sets the maximum _interval_ to wait for each DATA block read to complete (see §34.8.70.3, or define confTO_DATABLOCK with the _m4_ technique).

Timeout.datafinal=_interval_

> Sets the maximum _interval_ to wait for acknowledgment of the final dot that terminates the DATA phase (see §34.8.70.4, or define confTO_DATAFINAL with the _m4_ technique).

Timeout.datainit=_interval_

> Sets the maximum _interval_ to wait for acknowledgment of the SMTP DATA command (see §34.8.70.5, or define confTO_DATAINIT with the _m4_ technique).

Timeout.fileopen=_wait_

> Specifies how long to _wait_ for an NFS-mounted file to open (see §34.8.70.6, or define confTO_FILEOPEN with the _m4_ technique).

Timeout.helo=_interval_

> Sets the maximum _interval_ to wait for acknowledgment of the SMTP HELO or EHLO commands (see §34.8.70.7, or define confTO_HELO with the _m4_ technique).

Timeout.hoststatus=_interval_

> Specifies the _interval_ for which persistent host status should be considered still valid (see §34.8.70.8, or define confTO_HOSTSTATUS with the _m4_ technique).

Timeout.iconnect=_interval_

> Sets the maximum _interval_ to wait for the first _connect_(2) system call to complete (see §34.8.70.9, or define confTO_ICONNECT with the _m4_ technique).

Timeout.ident=_interval_

> Sets the maximum _interval_ to wait for the RFC1413 identification protocol to complete (see §34.8.70.10, or define confTO_IDENT with the _m4_ technique).

Timeout.initial=*interval*

> Sets the maximum *interval* to wait for the initial
> SMTP greeting message (see §34.8.70.11, or define
> `confTO_INITIAL` with the *m4* technique).

Timeout.mail=*interval*

> Sets the maximum *interval* to wait for acknowledg-
> ment of the SMTP MAIL command (see §34.8.70.12, or
> define `confTO_MAIL` with the *m4* technique).

Timeout.misc=*interval*

> Sets the maximum *interval* to wait for acknowledg-
> ment of SMTP commands, other than those specifi-
> cally mentioned here (see §34.8.70.13, or define
> `confTO_MISC` with the *m4* technique).

Timeout.queuereturn[.[*|urgent|normal|non-
urgent]]=*interval*

> Sets the maximum *interval* to try to deliver a mes-
> sage. The first time it fails after this interval, it is
> bounced. Three optional keywords can follow to
> what is bounced. They correspond to values given
> in a message's `Priority:` header. The literal ".*"
> is a wildcard that encompasses all three keywords
> (see §34.8.70.14, or define one of `confTO_`
> `QUEUERETURN`, `confTO_QUEUERETURN_` NONUR-
> GENT, `confTO_QUEUERETURN_NORMAL`, or
> `confTO_QUEUERETURN_URGENT` with the *m4* tech-
> nique).

Timeout.queuewarn[.[*|urgent|normal|non-
urgent]]=*interval*

> Causes a warning to be sent to the sender when a
> message is still undelivered after this *interval*. Three
> optional keywords can follow as described above
> (see §34.8.70.15, or define one of `confTO_`
> `QUEUEWARN`, `confTO_QUEUEWARN_NONURGENT`,
> `confTO_QUEUEWARN_NORMAL`, or `confTO_`
> `QUEUEWARN_URGENT` with the *m4* technique).

Timeout.quit=*interval*

> Sets the maximum *interval* to wait for acknowledgment of the SMTP QUIT command (see §34.8.70.16, or define `confTO_QUIT` with the *m4* technique).

Timeout.rcpt=*interval*

> Sets the maximum *interval* to wait for acknowledgment of the SMTP RCPT command (see §34.8.70.17, or define `confTO_RCPT` with the *m4* technique).

Timeout.rset=*interval*

> Sets the maximum *interval* to wait for acknowledgment of the SMTP RSET command (see §34.8.70.18, or define `confTO_RSET` with the *m4* technique).

Rule Sets

Rule sets are declared in the configuration file by beginning a line with the letter S:

```
Snumber
Sname
Sname=number
```

Rule sets are identified either by *number* or symbolic *name*. When identified by name, a number is internally assigned by *sendmail*. An optional = and number may follow a name to force specific association of number to name.

Rule sets numbered 0 through 9 are reserved for *sendmail's* internal use. Addresses are rewritten by a specific sequence of rules numbered 0 through 4 (see Figure 2-1).

S3   Rewrites all addresses to prepare them for entry into the sequence for rule sets. It usually focuses on the host part of an address and detects the various forms of the local hostname, so that local delivery can take place (see §29.4).

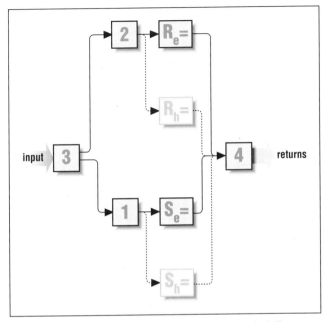

Figure 2-1: Sequence of rule sets; envelope (solid) versus header (dashed)

S4   Undoes any special rewriting done by rule set 3.
      Rule set 4 is always last (see §29.5).

S0   Selects a delivery agent that determines the **R=** and
      S= rule sets. It also selects the recipient user (which
      is separately rewritten and placed into **$u**) and the
      recipient host (which is placed as-is into **$h**). (See
      §.29.6)

S1   Rewrites all sender addresses (see §29.9).

S2   Rewrites all recipient addresses (see §29.8).

S5   (Not shown in Figure 2-1.) Can select a new deliv-
        ery agent (just like rule set 0). If the address is *not*
        matched in the *aliases*(5) database, it is passed to
        rule set 5. Addresses are given to rule set 5 before
        ˜/.forward files are processed (see §29.7).

Delivery Agent S= and R=

The S= rule set follows rule set 1 and rewrites the sender
address; the R= rule set follows rule set 2 and rewrites the
recipient address (see Figure 2-1). They are declared inside a
delivery agent declaration like this:

    S=*set*
    S=*eset/hset*
    R=*set*
    R=*eset/hset*

When there is just a single *set* specified, it is the rule set used
to rewrite both header and envelope addresses. When a slash
is present, the rule set to the left rewrites the envelope and
the one to the right, the headers. If any is missing or zero,
that rewriting is skipped.

Any S= rule set may be expressed as:

    number
    name
    name=number

When identified by name, a number is internally assigned by
sendmail. An optional = and number may follow a name to
force specific association of number to name.

The check_ Rule Sets

V8.8 *sendmail* has introduced a suite of named rule sets that
have special internal meaning. If one of these rule sets does
not exist, the address is accepted. If it exists and if the rule
set returns anything other than an `#error` delivery agent, the
message is accepted. Otherwise the message is rejected.

check_compat

>   Compares or contrasts each envelope sender and
>   envelope recipient pair of addresses just before
>   delivery, and validates based on the result. The
>   workspace looks like this:
>
>   *hostname* $| *IPnumber*
>
>   The hostname is separated from the IP number by a
>   single token that is the $| operator (see §29.10.4).

check_mail

>   Validates the sender-envelope address as given in
>   the SMTP MAIL command. The workspace, on entry,
>   contains a hostname that should be preprocessed by
>   rule set 3 (see §29.10.1).

check_rcpt

>   Validates the recipient-envelope address as given in
>   the SMTP RCPT command. The workspace, on entry,
>   contains a hostname that should be preprocessed by
>   rule set 3 (see §29.10.2).

check_relay

>   Validates incoming network connections and can be
>   used if *libwrap.a* code was omitted from your
>   release of *sendmail*. The workspace looks like this:
>
>   *hostname* $| *IPnumber*
>
>   The hostname is separated from the IP number by a
>   single token that is the $| operator (see §29.10.3).

Rules

Rules are declared in the configuration file with the **R** command:

R*LHS* tabs RHS [*tabs* COMMENT]

Rules are composed of two parts separated by *tab* characters (an optional third part can follow the first two, also separated by *tab* characters, and it forms a comment that is ignored).

Each rule forms a do-while statement as shown in Figure 2-2. So long as the LHS evaluates to true, the RHS rewrites the current address in the workspace. LHS evaluation is done by matching wildcard expressions to addresses. RHS rewriting is done by positional substitution. In this chapter we describe the wildcard and positional operators that aid in the writing of rules (see §28.1).

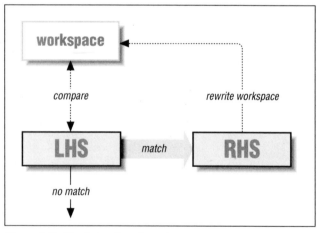

Figure 2-2: The behavior of a rule

Wildcard Operators in the LHS

The LHS of a rule is compared to an address or to the result of rewriting by earlier rules. The comparison is case insensitive. To illustrate, consider passing the address *hat@coat.org* to this LHS:

    $* @ $+ .ORG

The $* (match zero or more) will match *hat*, the @ will match exactly, the $+ (match one or more) will match *coat*, and the .ORG will match *.org* despite the case difference.

Wildcard operators match as little as possible in order to make the entire LHS match. For an address like *a@b@c*, the LHS $*@$+ will cause the $* to match the *a*.

$*
:   Matches zero or more tokens. Prefers zero, or the fewest possible, to satisfy an LHS match.

$+
:   Matches one or more tokens. Prefers one, or the fewest possible, to satisfy an LHS match.

$-
:   Matches exactly one token.

$@
:   Matches exactly zero tokens.

$=
:   Matches any word in a class. Words may be single-token (like *coat*) or multi-token (like *coat.org*).

$~
:   Matches any single token not in a class.

Positional Operators in the RHS

The RHS rewrites by substitution. Wildcard operators in the LHS select the portions of the workspace to be passed to the RHS. The first wildcard is assigned to $1, the second to $2, and so on. Consider:

    R$+@$* $2!$1
      ↑ ↑
     $1 $2

Here, an Internet address is rewritten in UUCP form. Note that there are only nine such positional operators, and that **$0** is illegal.

Other Operators in the RHS

Other operators in the RHS aid in rewriting. The first two below are prefixes, which means they must be the first operator in the RHS to have the desired effect. The others are more complex and may appear anywhere in the RHS.

$:   When used as a prefix, proceeds directly to the next *rule* immediately after the RHS rewrite without trying the LHS again.

$@   When used as a prefix, causes the current *rule set* to immediately return the result of the RHS rewrite without trying the LHS again (the current rule set exits).

$> *set tokens*
    Passes the *tokens* that follow through another rule *set*. The entire expression is replaced with the result of that subroutine call.

$[*host* $]
    Canonicalizes the hostname contained between this pair of operators. The result is placed into the workspace, and the operators dropped.

$(*key database* $: *default* $)
    Looks up the *key* in the *database* (see Chapter 3, *Databases*).

Operators that Return a Triple

Rule sets 0 and 5 are special in that they allow you to select a delivery agent. Selecting a delivery agent means placing a "triple" in the RHS. The form of that triple looks like this:

$# *agent* $@ *host* $: *user*

The order is important; any other order will fail.

$# *agent*

Selects the delivery *agent* by symbolic name. If the name is **error**, the message is bounced (or deferred) and the nature of the $@ and $: changes.

$@ *host* Selects the host to which the mail will be sent. The hostname is placed as-is into **$h**. For the **error** agent, this is the DSN return code (common codes are: 5.1.3 for illegal syntax, 5.1.1 for an address syntax error, 5.1.2 for an invalid hostname, or 5.7.1 for a security rejection; see RFC1893 and §30.5.2).

$: *user* Specifies the name of the recipient user. For remote mail this may be a full address. For local mail it may be a login name. The user name is processed by rule set 2, then by the rule set indicated by the **R=** equate of the delivery agent, then by rule set 4, and the result placed into **$u**. For the **error** agent, this is the literal text of the error message. A three-digit SMTP error code can optionally prefix this text (see §30.5.2).

Conditional Operators

Conditional operators allow text to be inserted that depends on the value in a macro. Conditional operators are never used in rules, but are often used in header definitions (see §31.6).

```
$?macro result $| alternate $.
```

If the *macro* has a value, the entire expression is replaced by *result*. Otherwise, the entire expression is replaced by *alternate*. For example:

```
From: $?x$x <$g>$|$g$.
```

Here, if **$x** has a value (the **$?x**), the entire expression becomes:

```
From: $x <$g>
```

Otherwise (the **$|$g**), it becomes:

```
From: $g
```

The **$.** is last and terminates the conditional expression. Conditional expressions may nest, but nesting is discouraged.

Hints

a new *sendmail.cf* **file**

> Requires that you restart the *sendmail* daemon, or else the daemon will not know of the changes. Before installing a new configuration file be sure to test it with the –C command-line switch. When using –C for testing, also use –oQ/tmp.

$=w and MX records

> Require that any host that lists your host as the best MX record be included in your hosts' **$=w** class declaration, or in your *sendmail.cw* file.

F=m and quotas

> Don't combine well. If one user is over quota, */bin/mail* cannot tell if one or all recipients of a multi-recipient message failed, so it exits in a way that causes *sendmail* to retry delivery to all the recipients over and over again. If you run quotas on the mail spool directory, try disabling the **F=m** flag for the local delivery agent.

Chapter 2: The sendmail.cf File

3

Databases

Database support in *sendmail* includes external files, internal symbol tables, and database-style hooks into processes. Databases support the common *aliases* and such *m4* style features as *mailertable* and the User Database.

Support in Makefile

Some database support is always supplied as a part of *sendmail* (like **dequote**), while others require you to include support inside your *Makefile* when building *sendmail*. Support is added on the DBMDEF= line:

```
DBMDEF= -DNDBM
```

This line adds support for *ndbm*(3) database files (see §18.4.1). Some database formats, such as *db*, may require that you also add include file and library support:

```
INCDIRS=-I/usr/local/include/db
LIBS=   -ldb -lresolv
```

Here LIBS= had −ldb added (see §18.4.6), and INCDIR= show the path to the *db* include files (see §18.4.3).

-DHESIOD
> Supports *hesiod*(3) for aliases only (see §18.8.10).

-DLDAPMAP
> Supports *ldap*(3) white pages (see §18.8.15).

-DNDBM

> Supports *ndbm*(3) database files (see §18.8.24).

-DNEWDB

> Supports the Berkeley *db*(3) database (see §18.8.28).

-DNIS Supports Sun's *nis* network services (see §18.8.29).

-DNISPLUS

> Supports Sun's *nisplus* network services (see §18.8.30).

-DNETINFO

> Supports NeXT's *netinfo*(3) (see §18.8.27).

Aliasing

The source and type of aliases are controlled by the
`AliasFile` option and the `aliases` entry in the service-
switch file. Alias entries are built from key and value pairs
where the key (the *list* name) is on the left, followed by a
colon, then by one or more *members* that form the value (see
§24.1):

> *list: member1, member2, . . .*

The sequence of *members* can be continued on subsequent
lines by beginning each such continuation line with white
space.

> *list: member1, member2,*
> *member3, member4, . . .*

Each list *member* may be a user address, a file name, a program reference, or a `:include:` reference.

addresses

> Are either standard email addresses (a local user or
> alias name or a *user@host*, where comments and
> "*Full Name <user@host>*" syntaxes are acceptable),
> or a local user name prefixed with a backslash
> (which forces immediate delivery, see §24.2.1).

---

files
Are specified by prefixing the file name with a forward slash (e.g., */path/file*); thus all file specifications must be full pathnames. Files must be world writable, or must have the *setuid* bit set but no execute bits set. Delivery is made by appending the message to the *file* (see §24.2.2).

programs
Are specified by prefixing the program with a vertical bar (e.g., |*/path/program*). If the program's invocation includes command-line arguments, it must be quoted. Programs are run as the sender (if local) or the default user (set by the `DefaultUser` option). Delivery is made by piping the message through the *program* (see §24.2.3).

`:include:`
Says that additional aliases will be read from a specified *file*, which must be a full pathname:

> `:include:` */path/file*

The file listed in a `:include:` reference must be world readable. The syntax of a file is identical to the syntax of a *.forward* file (described below). The owner of the `:include:` file is used for the permissions for writing files, running programs, and reading recursive `:include:` files (see §25.2).

Aliases are not processed until the alias database is rebuilt using the **newaliases** command or the **-bi** command-line switch (see §24.5.1).

The ~/.forward file

Users can redirect mail addressed to themselves by creating a file named *.forward* in their home directory (see §25.7). (The `ForwardPath` option is used to change or augment the location and name of the *.forward* file.) The *.forward* file must

---

be owned by the user or by *root*, and must *not* be world writable (mode 644 is recommended). Entries read:

    member1, member2, . . .

There can be multiple lines, but they are treated independently (there are no continuation lines). Just as in the *aliases* file, *members* may be a user address, a file name, a program reference, or a `:include:` reference. Files must be writable by the forwarding user, programs are run as the forwarding user, and `:include:` files must be readable by the forwarding user.

The ability to run progams or to write to files from the *.forward* file is controlled by the */etc/shells* file. If the owner of the *.forward* file lacks a valid shell as listed in */etc/shells*, program execution is disallowed. The special string */SENDMAIL/ANY/SHELL/*, when placed in the */etc/shells* file, allows all users to execute programs and deliver to files (see §18.8.56).

:include: *Files and Mailing Lists*

Files referenced using the `:include:` syntax have the same syntax as *˜/.forward* files. Any files written via a `:include:` file must be writable by the owner of the `:include:` file, and any other `:include:` files referenced for inclusion must be readable by the owner of the referencing `:include:` file.

To set up a mailing list managed by, for example, *sally*, set up the following aliases:

```
sample:           :include:/var/lists/sample.list
sample-request: sally
owner-sample:   sample-request
```

Then create the file */var/lists/sample.list*, mode 644, and owned by *sally*. Mail sent to *sample* will be sent to everyone on the list. Error messages will go directly to *sample-request*, and in turn to *sally*. (The *list-request* syntax is an Internet convention, see §25.2.)

The makemap Program

The *makemap*(1) program (part of *sendmail*'s source) is useful for producing database files. It supports the *ndbm*(3) form of database, and the *hash* and *btree* forms of the Berkeley *db*(3) database (see §33.2).

```
makemap switches class database
```

The *makemap*(1) program reads from its standard input lines of text with the key preceding the value on each line. Output is to *database* file. The *class* is selected from dbm, btree, or hash. The *switches* are:

-d   Allows duplicate keys. Without this switch, duplicate keys cause warnings to be printed (see §33.2.1.1).

-f   Prevents (the default) folding of keys from upper- to lowercase (see §33.2.1.2).

-N   Appends a null byte to all keys (see §33.2.1.3).

-o   Prevents *file* from being truncated on *open*(2). In other words, append to, don't overwrite the file (see §33.2.1.4).

-r   Replaces (silently) a duplicate key's value with the new value (see §33.2.1.5).

-v   Sets verbose mode so that you can watch keys and data being added (see §33.2.1.6).

The K Command

The **K** command is used to declare a database support in the configuration file:

```
Kname class switches database
```

The *name* is the symbolic name used in rule sets with the $(
and $) operators. The *class* is described in the next section.
The *switches* are described immediately below. The *database*
is either the name of an external database (possibly created
with *makemap*), or that of a flat text file (see §33.3).

-A   Appends values for duplicate keys (see §33.3.4.1).

-a *tag* Appends *tag* on a successful match (see §33.3.4.2).

-f   Prevents folding of keys to lowercase prior to the
          lookup (see §33.3.4.3).

-k *column*
          Specifies the *column* for the key in flat text or some
          network files (see §33.3.4.4).

-m   Suppresses replacement on match (see §33.3.4.5).

-N   Appends a null byte to the key before the lookup
          (see §33.3.4.6).

-O   Causes *sendmail* to not add a null byte to the key
          before the lookup. Note that with neither -O nor -N,
          sendmail determines adaptively whether or not it
          should add a null byte (see §33.3.4.7).

-o   Specifies that the existence of the database file is
          optional (see §33.3.4.8).

-q   Prevents quotes from being stripped from the key
          before the lookup (see §33.3.4.9).

-s *character*
          Specifies the space replacement *character* (see
          §33.3.4.10).

-v *column*
          Specifies the value's *column* for flat or some net-
          work files (see §33.3.4.11).

-z *delimiter*
          Specifies the column *delimiter* for flat or some net-
          work files (see §33.3.4.12).

Classes

There are many classes available for use with the **K** command and for use in rewriting rules. Some require special compile flags to be included when *sendmail* is built.

btree   Uses Berkeley's *db* form of database. Database file names have a *.db* appended (see §33.8.1).

bestmx   Looks up the best MX record for a host (see §33.8.2).

dbm   Uses the *ndbm* form of database. The database is formed of two files, one whose name ends in *.pag* and the other in *.dir* (see §33.8.3).

dequote   Removes quotation marks (see §33.8.4).

hash   Uses Berkeley's *db* form of database (see §33.8.5).

hesiod   Uses MIT network user authentication services (see §33.8.6).

host   Uses an internal table to store and look up host-names (see §33.4.3).

implicit   Searches for an *aliases* database file (see §33.8.8).

ldapx   Uses the Lightweight Directory Access Protocol (see §33.8.9).

netinfo   Uses NeXT Computer's network information services (see §33.8.10).

nis   Uses Sun's Network Information Services (*nis*, see §33.8.11).

nisplus   Uses Sun's newer Network Information Services (*nisplus*, see §33.8.12).

null   Provides a "never found" service (for internal use only, see §33.8.13).

program
    Runs an external program to look up the key (see §33.8.14).

---

sequence
> Searches a series of maps (see §33.8.15).

stab   Loads aliases into the symbol table (internally) (see §33.8.16).

switch Auto-builds sequences of databases based on service-switch file entries (see §33.8.17).

text   Looks up keys in flat text files (see §33.8.18).

userdb Uses the User Database (see §33.8.19).

user   Looks up local *passwd*(5) information (see §33.8.20).

Databases in Rules

Databases are accessed inside the RHS of rules with the **$(** and **$)** operators:

    $(key name $)

This looks up *key* in the database named *name* and replaces the entire expression (operators and all) with the value found in the database. If no value is found, the *key* replaces the expression, unless a **$:** gives a default:

    $(key name $: default $)

in which instance the *default* replaces the entire expression.

Optional replacement text can be appear between the *name* and the **$:** (if one) or the **$)**. Each is of the form "**$@***text*":

    $(key name $@text1 $@text2 $)
    $(key name $@text1 $@text2 $: default $)

The first (the **$@***text1*) will replace any literal %1 expressions in the value returned by the database. The second (the **$@***text2*) will replace %2, and so on. In this scheme, %0 always references the *key*. But note that not all map classes do this replacement.

The User Database

Locates mail drops when mail is received, and maps user names to their external form when mail is sent. The format of the database file (e.g., */etc/userdb*) is:

```
user:maildrop       user@host
user:mailname       alias@external.domain
```

As a shorthand, if all users in a database should have their domain name changed when mail is sent, use:

```
:default:mailname    external.domain
user1:maildrop       user1@host
user2:maildrop       user2@host
```

You build the database using the *makemap*(1) program:

```
% makemap btree /etc/userdb < /etc/userdb
```

Berkeley database (**btree** class) support is required.

Hints

-f and -N

> Must match between the configuration file's **K** line
> and the command-line run to execute *makemap*(1).
> But note that in most cases you probably don't want
> to use either switch.

text class

> Lookups on heavily loaded systems can be very
> slow. They can also be slow when the text file is
> extremely large. In either instance try to convert to
> an *ndbm-* or *db*-style database.

4

Configuring with m4

A configuration file is generated from an *m4* source file (e.g., one named *our.mc*) in the *cf/cf sendmail* source tree like this:

```
m4  ../m4/cf.m4 our.mc > sendmail.cf
```

To use a directory other than `../m4`, use:

```
m4 -D_CF_DIR_=path/ path/m4/cf.m4 our.mc >
    sendmail.cf
```

Here, *path* is the full path to the *m4/cf.m4* file. The *our.mc* source may contain the following lines (in this order):

```
OSTYPE(os)
DOMAIN(domain)
                         ← declare local parameters using
                            define here
FEATURE(feature)         ← can be several
MAILER(agent)            ← can be several
                         ← local rule set declarations here
```

Thus, a minimal file would declare the operating system and local delivery agent support with two lines like this:

```
OSTYPE(os)
MAILER(local)
```

In some cases you may see lines terminated with **dnl**, which means "delete to new line." Its use prevents extra blank lines from appearing in the output. It is almost never required. For more details about the *m4* technique in general, see §19.2.

OSTYPE

Causes support to be included from one of the files in the *cf/ostype* directory.

```
OSTYPE(os)
```

This sets defaults for your operating system from the file *cf/ostype/os.m4* (as for example, *sunos4.1.m4*). If you want to change any of the defaults that come with your operating system's file, do so after declaring OSTYPE. (See §19.3.1).

DOMAIN

Collects together local paramater declarations for an (optional) administrative domain:

```
DOMAIN(domain)
```

Here, *domain* is the name of a file in the *cf/domain* directory. With the exception of the file called *generic*, you should create your own *domain* file (see §19.3.3).

local parameter declarations

Are (mostly) named conf*NAME*, and most all cases are declared using the **define** directive:

```
define(`parameter_name', `value')
```

the *parameter_name*s define options and macros (see Chapter 2, *The sendmail.cf File*). In some cases local parameters are declared using special macros; see the next section.

FEATURE

Supplies simple solutions to special needs. The FEATURE directive is described below.

MAILER Causes support for delivery agents to be included. It must follow local parameter declarations because some of them change how a MAILER directive will be interpreted. MAILER is detailed following the features.

local rule set declarations

Allow you to easily add rules and rule sets to your
configuration file. Each definition stands on a line
by itself, and the lines following each are included
in the appropriate place in the configuration file. For
example: LOCAL_CONFIG to add general declarations
(e.g., **K** configuration databases) that should go at
the top of the configuration file (see §19.6.30);
LOCAL_RULE_0 to add rules to rule set 0 (see
§19.6.32); LOCAL_RULE_1 to add rules to rule set 1
(see §19.6.33); LOCAL_RULE_2 to add rules to rule set
2 (see §19.6.34); LOCAL_RULE_3 to add rules to rule
set 3 (see §19.6.35); and LOCAL_RULESETS to declare
entirely new rule sets, such as **check_relay** (see
§19.6.36).

Also select from: LOCAL_NET_CONFIG (used in con-
junction with LOCAL_RELAY) to add rules that tell
what addresses should *not* be forwarded to the relay
(see §19.6.37); and MAILER_DEFINITIONS to define
new delivery agents and the rule sets associated
with them (see §19.6.40).

Special Local Parameters

These lines should go in the DOMAIN file or before FEATURE
declarations (because they precondition certain features).

EXPOSED_USER(*user*)

(Used with MASQUERADE_AS) tells what users should
not be masqueraded (see §19.6.4).

GENERICS_DOMAIN(*domain*)

Lists the names of domains that will be looked up
with the **genericstable** feature. Declare one *domain*
per line. There may be several such lines.

GENERICS_DOMAIN_FILE(*file*)

> Specifies the *file* that contains the domains that will be looked up with the **genericstable** feature.

MASQUERADE_AS(*domain*)

> Causes all outgoing addresses to be rewritten as though they came from the indicated *domain* (see §19.6.42).

MASQUERADE_DOMAIN(*domain*)

> Specifies additional *domain*s that will be translated into the MASQUERADE_AS domain. See also the **limited_masquerade** feature (see §19.6.43).

MASQUERADE_DOMAIN_FILE(*file*)

> Specifies the name of the *file* that contains a list of domains that will be masqueraded (see §19.6.44).

FEATURE Declarations

In addition to minimal support, many handy features can be included with a line like:

    FEATURE (*feature*)

Here, *feature* is selected from those listed below. Some accept additional arguments. See *cf/README*, and §19.3.4, for details.

allmasquerade

> Causes the MASQUERADE_AS host to replace all header-recipient addresses too (see §19.6.6).

always_add_domain

> Tells *sendmail* to always append the local domain to addresses that lack a domain part, even if the recipient is local (see §19.6.7).

bestmx_is_local

> Accepts a hostname as local if the best MX record for that host is found in the class **$=w** (see §19.6.8).

bitdomain

Includes rules that support an external database for converting BITNET addresses into Internet addresses (see §19.6.9).

domaintable

Allows use of multiple domain names during a transition period (see §19.6.10).

genericstable

Includes rules that support use of a User Database-like facility to change recipient addresses so that recipients can be delivered to new hosts (see §19.6.11).

limited_masquerade

Specifies that only hosts declared with MASQUERADE_DOMAIN and MASQUERADE_DOMAIN_FILE may be masqueraded (see §19.6.12).

local_procmail

Includes rules that allow *procmail*(1) to be used as the local delivery agent (see §19.6.13).

mailertable

Includes rules that support a database that maps *host.domain* names to special delivery agents and new domain name pairs. Essentially it provides a database hook into rule set 0. The new domain names are used for routing but are not reflected in the headers of messages (see §19.6.14).

masquerade_entire_domain

Causes all hosts under any domains declared by MASQUERADE_DOMAIN or MASQUERADE_DOMAIN_FILE to be masqueraded. Ordinarily, masquerading only transforms hosts from a list of hosts in the class **$=w** (see §19.6.15).

masquerade_envelope

>   Causes the envelope to be masqueraded too. Ordinarily, masquerading only affects the headers (see §19.6.16).

nocanonify

>   Prevents *sendmail* from passing addresses to $[and $] for canonicalization. Ordinarily, as part of rule set 3, *sendmail* tries to canonify (add a domain to) any hostname that lacks a domain part (see §19.6.17).

nodns   Once caused DNS support to be excluded from the configuration file, but now does nothing. Deprecated; use the `ServiceSwitchFile` instead (see §19.6.18).

nouucp   Excludes UUCP support from the configuration file (see §19.6.19).

nullclient

>   Produces a minimal configuration file that can only forward mail to a mail hub machine (see §19.6.20).

redirect   Adds support for *address.REDIRECT* forms of addresses. This is chiefly used to bounce retired-account mail with useful forwarding information (see §19.6.21).

smrsh   Cause *smrsh(1)* (sendmail restricted shell) to be used in place of */bin/sh* as the shell for the **prog** delivery agent (see §19.6.22).

stickyhost

>   Causes all addresses without a host part to be forwarded to a central mail server, while allowing those with a local host part to remain on the local machine and be delivered in the usual local way (see §19.6.24).

use_ct_file

> Causes a list of trusted users to be read from the
> */etc/sendmail.ct* file (see §19.6.25).

use_cw_file

> Causes a list of local hostnames to be read from the
> */etc/sendmail.cw* file (see §19.6.26).

uucpdomain

> Includes rules that cause hostnames of the form
> *host.UUCP* to be looked up in a database. If found,
> they are rewritten to an *@host* form as specified in
> that database (see §19.6.27).

virtusertable

> Maps virtual (possibly nonexistent) domains into
> new addresses. Note that this reroutes delivery, but
> does not change the mail headers (see §19.6.28).

MAILER Declarations

Delivery agents are declared using the MAILER directive:

```
MAILER(agent)
```

The available *agent*s are listed in the *cf/mailer* directory (see
§19.3.2). For example, consider:

```
MAILER(local)
MAILER(smtp)
```

Here, the first includes support for local delivery, delivery to
files, and delivery through programs. The second allows the
sendmail daemon to accept incoming mail.

cyrus   Declares `cyrus` for delivery to the Cyrus IMAP4
server, and `cyrusbb` for delivery to a Cyrus bulletin
board.

fax   Declares `fax` for delivery to a mail-to-fax gateway.

local Declares `local` for delivery to a local mailbox and `prog` for delivery through a shell program.

mail11 Declares `mail11` for delivery to a DECnet/mail11 gateway.

phquery

Declares `ph`, which uses the *phquery* program to send to the *ph* directory service.

pop Declares `pop` for delivery through the MH *spop* program.

procmail

Declares `procmail` for delivery using the *procmail* program.

smtp Declares `smtp`, which handles SMTP mail; `esmtp`, which always speaks ESMTP instead of adapting on the basis of the greeting message; `smtp8`, which always uses sends-8-bit data directly; and `relay`, which uses SMTP with minimal rewriting and only works within a single domain.

usenet Declares `usenet` for delivery to a mail-to-news gateway.

uucp Declares `uucp-old`, `uucp-new`, `uucp-uudom`, and `uucp-dom`. Use `uucp-old` if your peers are running very old (V7) versions of UUCP. Use `uucp-new` if they are running a newer version (e.g., *honey danber*) but don't understand domain-based addressing. Use `uucp-uudom` if your peers use UUCP addresses (e.g., *host!user*) in the envelope, but domain-based addresses (*user@host.domain*) in the headers. Use `uucp-dom` if your peers are completely converted to domain-based addressing. The last two are only defined if MAILER(smtp) is declared before MAILER(uucp).

Virtual User Tables

When using FEATURE(virtusertable), *sendmail* will do transla-
tion based on the entire domain name when the address is
first read. This is similar, but not identical, to aliasing. It is
commonly used to host multiple domains with different (and
possibly even overlapping) users on one machine using MX
records. The format of the input file (e.g., */etc/virtusertable*)
is:

> [*virtuser*]@*virtdomain   address*

For example, an input file might read:

```
info@foo.com       foo-info
info@bar.com       bar-info
john@foo.com       jdoe
jane@foo.com       jroe@elsewhere.com
@bar.com           mary
```

The first two entries translate *info@foo.com* and *info@bar.com*
into different names, which may be user names or aliases.
The third and fourth entries alias users to other names. The
fifth entry says that *anything@bar.com* that wasn't otherwise
recognized should go to *mary*.

You build the database from the input file using the *makemap*(1) program:

```
% makemap hash /etc/virtusertable < /etc/virtusertable
```

You declare the database for use with your *.mc* file, like this:

```
FEATURE(virtusertable, hash /etc/virtusertable)
```

Mailer Tables

Mailer tables are a simple way of directing messages to different Mail Delivery Agents (MDAs) on the basis of host or domain names. For example, consider this input file (e.g., */etc/mailertable*):

```
remote.foo.com  uucp-uudom:home
.skunkworks.foo.com   relay:secret.foo.com
```

Here the first line says that anything addressed to *user@remote.foo.com* should be sent using the **uucp-uudom** deilvery agent to the host named *home*. The second line says that any message addressed to any host within the domain *.skunkworks.foo.com* should be sent using the **relay** delivery agent to the host *secret.foo.com*.

You can build the database from the input file using the *makemap*(1) program:

```
% makemap hash /etc/mailertable < /etc/mailertable
```

You declare the database for use with your *.mc* file, like this:

```
FEATURE(mailertable, hash /etc/mailertable)
```

Hints

- *Always test* your newly generated configuration file with *sendmail*'s (**-bt**) rule-testing mode. Run a series of predetermined addresses through the **/parse** command and look for any discrepencies that look odd.

- *Make sure your DOMAIN file* does *not* define operating system-dependent parameters. It should contain parameter and FEATURE declarations that you want *all* the machines in your domain to share. For example, if you want to include FEATURE(redirect) or FEATURE(nouucp), declare them in your DOMAIN file for consistency across all hosts in your domain.

- *A new binary* should always be accompanied by a new configuration file. Whenever you build a new version of *sendmail,* be sure to also create a new configuration file with the *m4* technique.

5

Additional Information Sources

No reference this tiny can contain all the information you need. The *sendmail* source comes with many useful documents.

RELEASE_NOTES
> Describes all the changes that have occured from version to version.

READ_ME
> Tells what is where in the source tree and gives a few cautionary general announcements.

src/READ_ME
> Describes how to edit *Makefile*, and how to build and install *sendmail*.

cf/README
> Describes how to create a configuration file using the *m4* technique.

doc/op Contains the *Installation and Operations Guide*. This directory contains the *–me* source and printer-ready PostScript.

FAQ   Included with the source, is deprecated. Instead look for the most current FAQ that is periodically posted to the Usenet newsgroups *comp.mail.sendmail* and *comp.answers*. A link to the latest archived FAQ can be found at *http://www.sendmail.org*.

In addition to these documents supplied with the source, you can always find the most up-to-the-minute information at **http://www.sendmail.org**.